# VEGETARIAN COOKING

Photography by Peter Barry
Recipes styled by Helen Burdett
Designed by Richard Hawke
Edited by Jillian Stewart
3258
© 1993 Coombe Books
This edition published in 1994 by Coombe Books for
Parragon Book Service Ltd
Unit 13-17, Avonbridge Trading Estate
Atlantic Road, Avonmouth, Bristol BS11 9QD
All rights reserved
Printed and bound in Hong Kong
ISBN 1-85813-135-9

# VEGETARIAN COOKING

PARRAGON

# Contents

# Introduction

Vegetarian cooking grows in popularity year by year as more and more people realise the health advantages of a meat-free diet. People choose to eat vegetarian meals for many different reasons, but whether it is for the sake of economising or on moral grounds, it can represent an important move towards a healthier lifestyle.

Contrary to what many people believe, vegetarian food does not have to be boring or complex. Products such as pasta, eggs, cheese, rice, beans, and fruit all play as important a part in a vegetarian diet as do vegetables, and they can be utilised to produce healthy, nutritious and interesting meals which will appeal to all ages and tastes.

The mention of vegetarian food often makes many people think of rather bland unappetising food that needs lengthy preparation and careful thought. This need not be so – vegetarian meals can be as simple or as complicated as you wish, and the general guidelines for good nutrition are simple. One of the main reasons why a vegetarian diet is considered to be healthy is that it cuts out cholesterol-rich red meat, but as red meat is a rich source of protein this has to be replaced and not simply left out.

There are many different of ways to add protein to a vegetarian diet. Undoubtedly the cheapest and one of the most valuable sources of protein are beans and pulses. Not only are they tasty, but they can be used to replace meat in a huge variety of dishes such as chillies, casseroles and terrines. Cheese and eggs can be incorporated in starters and desserts as well as main courses, although care must be taken not to eat too much rich, fatty cheese. One of the most useful advances in meat-free protein is the growth in popularity of products such as tofu, which is healthy, low in fat and, because it absorbs flavours well, can be adapted to a whole variety of dishes.

You will find a wealth of ideas within these pages to add interest to your weekly menus. So whether it is a quick snack or a family meal, these imaginative easy-to-follow recipes ensure that producing the perfect vegetarian dish is simplicity itself.

# CREAM OF CARROT SOUP

*A classic soup which is suitable for any occasion.*

*SERVES 4*

1 large onion, chopped
2 cloves garlic, crushed
1 tbsp olive oil
450g/1lb carrots, chopped
1 tsp mixed herbs
850ml/1½ pints stock
140ml/¼ pint soured cream
Salt and pepper

**1.** Sauté the chopped onion and garlic in the oil until transparent.

**2**. Add the carrots, mixed herbs and stock.

**3.** Bring to the boil and simmer for about 30 minutes until the carrots are soft.

**4.** Cool a little and then liquidise until smooth.

**5.** Add the soured cream, season to taste and mix thoroughly.

**6.** Heat through gently and serve.

TIME: Preparation takes about 10 minutes, cooking takes 35 minutes.

WATCHPOINT: Do not allow the soup to boil after adding the soured cream.

VARIATION: For a richer soup, omit the soured cream and add a swirl of double cream just before serving.

# WILD RICE SOUP

*A meal in itself when served with granary bread and a green salad.*

*SERVES 4*

---

50g/2oz wild rice
420ml/¾ pint water
2 onions, chopped
1 tbsp butter or ghee
2 sticks celery, chopped
½ tsp dried thyme
½ tsp dried sage
850ml/1½ pints water or vegetable stock
2 tsps Vecon (vegetable stock)
1 tbsp shoyu (Japanese soy sauce)
6 small potatoes, peeled and roughly
  chopped
1 carrot, finely diced
Milk or single cream

---

**1.** Add the wild rice to the water, bring to the boil, reduce the heat and simmer for 40-50 minutes until the rice has puffed and most of the liquid has been absorbed.

**2.** Sauté the onions in the butter until transparent.

**3.** Add the celery, thyme and sage and cook for 5-10 minutes.

**4.** Add the water, vecon, shoyu and potatoes.

**5.** Simmer for 20 minutes or until the potatoes are cooked.

**6.** Blend the mixture in a liquidiser until smooth.

**7.** Return to the pan, add the carrot and wild rice.

**8.** Add the milk or cream to thin the soup to the desired consistency.

**9.** Reheat gently and serve.

---

TIME: Preparation takes about 15 minutes. Cooking takes 30 minutes plus 40 minutes to cook the wild rice.

COOK'S TIP: You can prepare and cook the soup whilst the wild rice is cooking. Add the rice to the soup at the end of the cooking time.

FREEZING: Cook a large quantity of wild rice and freeze in small portions. Add to the soup or other dishes as needed.

VARIATION: Toast some flaked almonds and sprinkle on top of the soup before serving.

# FRENCH ONION SOUP

*This soup tastes best if cooked the day*
*before it is needed and then reheated as required.*

*SERVES 4*

3 medium onions
50g/2oz butter or margarine
25g/1oz plain flour or soya flour
1ltr/1¾ pints boiling vegetable stock or
    water plus 2 stock cubes
Salt and pepper

*Topping*
4 slices French bread, cut crosswise
50g/2oz Cheddar cheese, grated
25g/1oz Parmesan cheese, grated

**1.** Slice the onions very finely into rings.

**2.** Melt the butter in a pan, add the onion rings and fry over a medium heat until well browned.

**3.** Mix in the flour and stir well until browned.

**4.** Add the stock and seasoning and simmer for 30 minutes.

**5.** Toast the bread on both sides.

**6.** Combine the cheeses, divide the mixture between the bread slices and grill them until golden brown.

**7.** Place the slices of bread and cheese in the bottom of individual soup dishes and spoon the soup over the top.

**8.** Serve at once.

TIME: Preparation takes 10 minutes, cooking takes 30 minutes.

VARIATION: For a special occasion, add a tablespoonful of brandy to the stock.

WATCHPOINT: The onions must be very well browned, as this gives the rich colour to the soup.

# CAULIFLOWER AND BROCCOLI SOUFLETTES

*Serve as a winter-time starter or as a main meal with rice salad and ratatouille.*

*SERVES 6*

350g/12oz cauliflower
350g/12oz broccoli
50g/2oz margarine
50g/2oz brown rice flour
420ml/¾ pint milk
50g/2oz Cheddar cheese, grated
1 large egg, separated
Good pinch of nutmeg

**1.** Break the cauliflower and broccoli into small florets and steam until just tender - about 7-10 minutes.

**2.** Melt the margarine, remove from the heat and gradually add the flour. Stir to a roux and add the milk gradually, blending well to ensure a smooth consistency.

**3.** Return the pan to the heat and stir until the sauce thickens and comes to the boil.

**4.** Cool a little and add the egg yolk and cheese, stir well and add nutmeg to taste.

**5.** Whip the egg white until stiff and fold carefully into the sauce.

**6.** Place the vegetables into 6 small buttered ramekin dishes and season.

**7.** Divide the sauce evenly between the dishes and bake immediately at 190°C/375°F/Gas Mark 5 for about 35 minutes until puffed and golden.

**8.** Serve at once.

TIME: Preparation takes 15 minutes, cooking takes 50 minutes.

# Date, Apple and Celery Starter

*A healthy dish with a tasty mix of flavours.*

*SERVES 4*

2 dstsp desiccated coconut
2 crisp eating apples
3-4 sticks celery
75g/3oz dates
2 tbsps natural yogurt
Salt and pepper
Pinch of nutmeg

**1.** Toast the coconut in a dry frying pan over a low heat until it is golden brown, then put to one side.

**2.** Core and dice the apples and chop the celery finely.

**3.** Plunge the dates into boiling water, drain and chop finely.

**4.** Combine the apples, celery and dates in a mixing bowl.

**5.** Add the yogurt, seasoning and nutmeg and mix thoroughly so that the salad is coated completely.

**6.** Transfer to a serving bowl and garnish with the toasted coconut.

**7.** Serve at once.

TIME: Preparation takes 10 minutes, cooking takes 2-3 minutes.

SERVING IDEA: Serve individual portions on a bed of watercress.

COOK'S TIP: Red skinned apples add colour to this salad.

17

# INDONESIAN-STYLE STUFFED PEPPERS

*For this adaptable recipe you can substitute
pine nuts or peanuts if you don't have cashews.*

*SERVES 8 AS A STARTER*

30ml/2 tbsps olive oil
1 medium onion, peeled and chopped
1 clove garlic, crushed
2 tsps turmeric
1 tsp crushed coriander seed
2 tbsps dessicated coconut
100g/4oz mushrooms, chopped
75g/3oz bulgar wheat
50g/2oz raisins
25g/1oz creamed coconut
280ml/½ pint stock or water
200g/7oz tomatoes, skinned and chopped
50g/2oz cashew nuts
4 small green peppers, de-seeded and cut
   in half lenthways
2 tsps lemon juice
Stock for cooking

**1.** Heat the oil and fry the onion and garlic until lightly browned.

**2.** Add the turmeric, coriander and dessicated coconut and cook gently for about 2 minutes.

**3.** Add the mushrooms and bulgar wheat and cook for a further 2 minutes.

**4.** Add the rest of the ingredients except the nuts, lemon juice, peppers, and cooking stock, and simmer gently for 15-20 minutes until the bulgar wheat is cooked.

**5.** Toast the cashew nuts in a dry frying pan until golden brown.

**6.** Blanch the peppers in boiling water for 3 minutes.

**7.** Mix the nuts and lemon juice with the rest of the ingredients and fill the peppers with the mixture.

**8.** Place the filled peppers on the bottom of a large casserole dish and pour stock around the peppers.

**9.** Cook 180°C/350°F/Gas Mark 4 for 20 minutes.

**10.** Drain peppers and place on a hot plate to serve.

TIME: Preparation takes 20 minutes, cooking takes 45 minutes.

FREEZING: The cooked peppers will freeze well for up to 3 months.

# WATERCRESS AND MUSHROOM PÂTÉ

*A delightful pâté which is perfect garnished with lime
or lemon wedges and served with thinly
sliced brown bread and butter.*

*SERVES 4*

25g/1oz butter
1 medium onion, finely chopped
75g/3oz dark, flat mushrooms, finely
  chopped
1 bunch watercress, finely chopped
100g/4oz low fat curd cheese
Few drops shoyu sauce (Japanese soy
  sauce)
Scant ½ tsp caraway seeds
Black pepper

**1.** Melt the butter over a low heat and cook the onion until soft but not coloured.

**2.** Raise the heat, add the mushrooms and cook quickly for 2 minutes.

**3.** Put in the chopped watercress and stir for about 30 seconds until it becomes limp.

**4.** Place the contents of the pan in a blender together with the cheese and shoyu sauce.

**5.** Blend until smooth.

**6.** Stir in the caraway seeds and pepper to taste.

**7.** Put into individual ramekin dishes or one large serving dish and chill for at least 2 hours until firm.

TIME: Preparation takes 10 minutes, cooking takes 5 minutes.

COOK'S TIP: It may be necessary to stir the contents of the blender several times as the mixture should be fairly thick.

# BRAZILIAN AVOCADOS

*The perfect way to impress your dinner guests
right from the first course.*

*SERVES 4*

2 large ripe avocados
A little lemon juice
Salt and pepper
50g/2oz finely chopped Brazil nuts
50g/2oz Cheddar cheese, grated
2 tbsps Parmesan cheese
2 level tbsps freshly chopped parsley
2 firm ripe tomatoes, skinned and finely
    chopped
Wholemeal breadcrumbs
25g/1oz melted butter
A little paprika

**1.** Halve the avocados and carefully remove the flesh from the skins. Brush the inside of the skins with a little of the lemon juice.

**2.** Dice the avocado and put into a bowl with a sprinkling of lemon juice and the seasoning.

**3.** Add the nuts, cheeses, parsley and tomato.

**4.** Mix gently.

**5.** Spoon the filling into the avocado shells, sprinkle with the breadcrumbs and drizzle the butter over the top.

**6.** Dust with the paprika and bake at 200°C/400°F/Gas Mark 6 for 15 minutes.

TIME: Preparation takes about 10 minutes, cooking takes 15 minutes.

COOK'S TIP: Do not prepare this dish too far in advance as the avocado may discolour.

SERVING IDEA: Serve with a little salad as a starter or with baked potatoes, vegetables and tossed salad for a main course.

# SAVOURY TOMATOES

*An ideal starter for slimmers.*

*SERVES 4*

4 large Spanish tomatoes
4 tbsps cottage cheese
1 tsp ground cumin
1 green pepper, de-seeded and diced
Seasoning
50g/2oz pumpkin seeds
1 bunch watercress

**1.** Slice off the tops of the tomatoes.

**2.** Remove the seeds and leave upside down to drain.

**3.** Rub the cottage cheese through a sieve to achieve a smooth consistency, add a little milk if necessary.

**4.** Stir in the cumin, pepper and seasoning.

**5.** Divide the mixture into four and stuff the tomatoes.

**6.** Dry roast the pumpkin seeds in a frying pan until they are lightly browned. Sprinkle over the tomatoes.

**7.** Chill until required.

**8.** Serve on a bed of watercress.

TIME: Preparation takes 10 minutes.

SERVING IDEA: Serve with very thin slices of brown bread and butter.

VARIATION: Use cream cheese in place of the cottage cheese.

# MUSHROOMS AND TOFU IN GARLIC BUTTER

*A quick and delicious starter.*

*SERVES 4*

225g/8oz button mushrooms
2.5cm/1 inch piece root ginger
225g/8oz smoked tofu
100g/4oz butter
4 small cloves garlic, crushed
2 tbsps chopped parsley

**1.** Wipe the mushrooms with a damp cloth.

**2.** Peel and grate the root ringer.

**3.** Cut the smoked tofu into small 1.2cm./ ½ -inch squares.

**4.** Melt the butter in a frying pan.

**5.** Add the crushed garlic and ginger and fry gently for two minutes.

**6.** Add the mushrooms and cook gently for 4-5 minutes until the mushrooms are softened.

**7.** Finally, add the smoked tofu and heat through.

**8.** Divide between 4 individually heated dishes, sprinkle with chopped parsley and serve at once.

TIME: Preparation takes 10 minutes, cooking takes 12 minutes.

SERVING IDEA: Serve with French bread or crusty wholemeal rolls.

VARIATION: Substitute asparagus tips for the button mushrooms.

# SPICY BLACK-EYED BEANS

*A spicy dish from the West Indies – perfect as a snack.*

*SERVES 4*

225g/8oz black-eyed beans, soaked and cooked
4 tbsps vegetable oil
1 large onion, finely chopped
2 cloves garlic, crushed
1 tsp ground cinnamon
½ tsp ground cumin
Salt and pepper
140ml/¼ pint bean stock or water
2 tbsps tomato purée
1 tbsp shoyu sauce (Japanese soy sauce)
2 large tomatoes, skinned and chopped
1 tbsp chopped parsley

**1.** Drain the beans well and retain the cooking liquid.

**2.** Heat the oil and fry the onion and garlic for 4-5 minutes until soft.

**3.** Stir in the cinnamon, cumin and seasoning and cook for a further 2 minutes.

**4.** Add the beans, bean stock, tomato purée, shoyu sauce and tomatoes.

**5.** Stir and bring to the boil.

**6.** Simmer for 15-20 minutes until thick.

**7.** Check the seasoning.

**8.** Sprinkle with chopped parsley and serve.

TIME: Preparation takes 20 minutes. Cooking time, including the beans, 1 hour 35 minutes.

SERVING IDEA: Serve over cooked pasta.

VARIATION: Haricot beans can be used in place of black-eyed beans.

# MIXED NUT BALLS

*This versatile dish can be made in advance and
refrigerated until required for cooking.*
*SERVES 8*

60g/2½ oz ground almonds
60g/2½ oz ground hazelnuts
60g/2½ oz ground pecan nuts
75g/3oz wholemeal breadcrumbs
100g/4oz Cheddar cheese, grated
1 egg, beaten
4-5 tbsps dry sherry or 2 tbsps milk and 3
    tbsps dry sherry
1 small onion, finely chopped
1 tbsp grated fresh ginger
1 tbsp fresh parsley, chopped
1 small red or green chilli, finely chopped
1 medium red pepper, diced
1 tsp sea salt
1 tsp freshly ground black pepper

**1.** Mix the almonds, hazelnuts and pecan
nuts together with the breadcrumbs and
the cheese.

**2.** In another bowl, mix the beaten egg
with the sherry, onion, ginger, parsley,
chilli and red pepper.

**3.** Combine with the nut mixture and add
the salt and pepper.

**4.** If the mixture is too dry, add a little
more sherry or milk.

**5.** Form into small 2cm/1-inch balls.

**6.** Do not preheat the oven.

**7.** Arrange the balls on a well greased
baking tray and bake at 180°C/350°F/Gas
Mark 4 for about 20-25 minutes, until
golden brown.

TIME: Preparation takes about 20 minutes, cooking takes 20-25 minutes.

SERVING IDEA: Serve on individual plates on a bed of chopped lettuce. Garnish with slices
of lemon and hand round your favourite sauce in a separate bowl.

# PEANUT RISOTTO

*Use this mixture to stuff cabbage, spinach or vine leaves or serve as a snack.*

*SERVES 4*

1 large onion, chopped
1 clove garlic, crushed
1 tbsp vegetable oil
150g/6oz short grain brown rice
100g/4oz peanuts, roughly chopped
100g/4oz mushrooms, sliced
570ml/1 pint boiling water
100g/4oz fine beans
25g/1oz raisins
2 tsps dried oregano
2 tsps lemon juice
Salt and pepper

**1.** Fry the onion and garlic in the oil for 3-4 minutes.

**2.** Add the rice and peanuts to toast for 1-2 minutes.

**3.** Add the mushrooms and cook for a further 3-4 minutes, then add the boiling water, stir once and simmer for 30 minutes.

**4.** Add the beans, raisins, herbs, lemon juice and seasoning and cook for a further 5-10 minutes.

TIME: Preparation takes 10 minutes, cooking takes 50 minutes.

SERVING IDEA: Serve garnished with lemon wedges and parsley.

VARIATION: Use this mixture to stuff cabbage, spinach or vine leaves.

# MUSHROOM CURRY

*An ideal snack or supper dish.*

*SERVES 4*

---

225g/8oz leeks, finely sliced
2 cloves garlic, crushed
½ tsp grated ginger
2 tsps curry powder
1 tsp garam masala
2 tbsps oil
450g/1lb mushrooms, cut into quarters
100g/4oz creamed coconut, grated
1 tbsp lemon juice

**1.** Fry the leeks, garlic, ginger and spices in the oil until soft.

**2.** Add the mushrooms and cook over a low heat until soft.

**3.** Add the grated coconut and cook gently until the coconut has completely dissolved, adding a little water if the mixture appears too dry.

**4.** Stir in the lemon juice and sufficient salt to taste.

**5.** Serve on a bed of rice.

---

TIME: Preparation takes 15 minutes, cooking takes about 20 minutes.

SERVING IDEA: Serve with a tomato and onion salad.

# PARSNIP FRITTERS

*These tasty fritters make a nice change for lunch or a light snack.*

*SERVES 4*

100g/4oz plain unbleached flour
2 tsps baking powder
1 tsp salt
½ tsp pepper
1 egg
140ml/¼ pint milk
1 tbsp melted butter
680g/1½lbs cooked parsnips, finely
   diced
Oil or clarified butter for frying

**1.** Sift together the flour, baking powder,
salt and pepper.

**2.** Beat the egg and mix with the milk and
melted butter.

**3.** Stir this mixture into the dry
ingredients.

**4.** Stir in the cooked parsnips.

**5.** Divide the mixture into 16 and shape
into small fritters.

**6.** Fry in oil or clarified butter until
browned on both sides.

TIME: Preparation takes 10 minutes, cooking takes about 5-8 minutes per batch.

VARIATION: Courgettes, sweetcorn, onions or aubergine may be
substituted for the parsnips.

SERVING IDEA: Serve with yogurt sauce or make them slightly larger
and serve as a main course with salad.

# BULGAR RISOTTO

*This makes a quick lunch dish and is
particularly handy if unexpected guests call.*

*SERVES 3-4*

100g/4oz bulgar wheat
1 medium onion, peeled and finely
  chopped
2 sticks celery, finely chopped
1-2 cloves garlic, crushed
12g/½ oz butter
1 small red pepper, diced
1 small green pepper, diced
½ tsp dried mixed herbs
50g/2oz peanuts, chopped
1 tsp vegetable extract dissolved in ¼ cup
  boiling water
2 tsps shoyu sauce (Japanese soy sauce)
75g/3oz sweetcorn
75g/3oz peas
Salt and pepper
Juice of half a lemon

**1.** Put the bulgar wheat into a bowl and
cover with boiling water.

**2.** Leave for about 10 minutes after which
time the water will have been absorbed
and the wheat swollen.

**3.** Meanwhile, place the onion, celery and
garlic into a saucepan and sauté for a few
minutes in the butter.

**4.** Add the peppers, herbs, nuts and
vegetable extract.

**5.** Simmer over a low heat for about 8
minutes.

**6.** Add the bulgar wheat, shoyu,
sweetcorn, peas and seasoning and mix
together well.

**7.** Continue cooking for a further 5
minutes.

**8.** Mix in the lemon juice and transfer to a
heated serving dish.

**9.** Serve immediately.

TIME: Preparation takes 15 minutes, cooking takes 20 minutes.

SERVING IDEA: Serve with a crisp green salad.

WATCHPOINT: If the risotto is too dry, add a little more water or stock.

# FLAGEOLET FIESTA

*Serve this dish on its own as a starter or as
a snack with lots of crusty bread.*

*SERVES 4*

225g/8oz flageolet beans, soaked
  overnight
1 medium onion
1 clove garlic
Half a cucumber
2 tbsps chopped parsley
2 tbsps chopped mint
2 tbsps olive oil
Juice and grated rind of 1 lemon
Salt
Freshly ground black pepper
Watercress to garnish

**1.** Cook the flageolet beans in plenty of
boiling water for about 1 hour or until just
tender.

**2.** Drain and put into a mixing bowl.

**3.** Peel and finely chop the onion.

**4.** Crush the garlic and chop the cucumber
into bite-sized pieces.

**5.** Add the onion, garlic, cucumber, herbs,
oil, lemon juice and rind to the beans and
mix well.

**6.** Add seasoning to taste and leave to
marinate for 2 hours.

**7.** Transfer to a clean serving bowl.

**8.** Serve garnished with watercress.

TIME: Preparation takes 15 minutes. Marinating takes 2 hours and cooking takes 1 hour.

VARIATION: Substitute red kidney beans for the flageolet beans.

# PASTA AND AVOCADO SALAD

*The perfect lunch or supper salad for guests.*

*SERVES 4*

225g/8oz pasta shapes
3 tbsps mayonnaise
2 tsps tahini
1 orange
½ medium red pepper, chopped
1 medium avocado
Pumpkin seeds to garnish

**1.** Cook the pasta until soft and leave to cool.

**2.** Mix together the mayonnaise and tahini.

**3.** Segment the orange and chop into small pieces, retain any juice.

**4.** Chop the pepper.

**5.** Stir the mayonnaise mixture, pepper and orange (plus juice) into the pasta.

**6.** Just before serving, cube the avocado and stir in carefully.

**7.** Serve on an oval dish, decorated with pumpkin seeds.

TIME: Preparation takes 10 minutes, cooking takes about 35 minutes.

WATCHPOINT: Do not peel the avocado until required as it may discolour.

VARIATION: Green pepper may be used in place of the red pepper.

# TABOULEH

*This is a traditional salad from the Middle East. The main
ingredient is bulgar which is partially cooked cracked wheat and
only needs soaking for a short while before it is ready to eat.*

*SERVES 6*

175-200g/6-7oz bulgar wheat
1 tsp salt
350ml/12fl.oz boiling water
450g/1lb tomatoes, chopped
½ cucumber, diced
3-4 spring onions

*Dressing*
50ml/2fl.oz olive oil
50ml/2fl.oz lemon juice
2 tbsps fresh mint
4 tbsps fresh parsley
2 cloves garlic, crushed

**1.** Mix the bulgar wheat with the salt, pour over the boiling water and leave for 15-20 minutes. All the water will then be absorbed.

**2.** Mix together the ingredients for the dressing and pour over the soaked bulgar.

**3.** Fold in lightly with a spoon.

**4.** Leave for two hours or overnight in a fridge or cool place.

**5.** Add the salad ingredients and serve.

TIME: Preparation takes about 20 minutes, standing time is about 2 hours.

COOK'S TIP: A few cooked beans can be added to make this dish more substantial.

SERVING IDEA: Serve with flans, cold pies and roasts.

# BAVARIAN POTATO SALAD

*It is best to prepare this salad a few hours in advance to allow the potatoes to absorb the flavours.*

*SERVES 4-6*

900g/2lbs tiny new potatoes
4 tbsps olive oil
4 spring onions, finely chopped
1 clove garlic, crushed
2 tbsps fresh dill, chopped or 1 tbsp dried
2 tbsps wine vinegar
½ tsp sugar
Seasoning
2 tbsps chopped fresh parsley

**1.** Wash the potatoes but do not peel, put them into a pan, cover with water and boil until just tender.

**2.** Whilst the potatoes are cooking, heat the olive oil in a frying pan and cook the spring onions and garlic for 2-3 minutes until they have softened a little.

**3.** Add the dill and cook gently for a further minute.

**4.** Add the wine vinegar and sugar, and stir until the sugar melts. Remove from the heat and add a little seasoning.

**5.** Drain the potatoes and pour the dressing over them whilst they are still hot.

**6.** Allow to cool and sprinkle with the chopped parsley before serving.

TIME: Preparation takes 15 minutes, cooking takes 15 minutes.

SERVING IDEA: Serve with cold roasts.

# WHEATBERRY SALAD

*This makes a substantial salad dish which provides an
almost perfect protein balance.*

*SERVES 4*

225g/8oz wheatberries, cooked
100g/4oz kidney beans, cooked
3 medium tomatoes
4 spring onions, chopped
2 sticks celery, chopped
1 tbsp pumpkin seeds

*Dressing*
4 tbsps olive or sunflower oil
2 tbsps red wine vinegar
1 clove garlic, crushed
1 tsp grated fresh ginger
1 tsp paprika
1 tbsp shoyu (Japanese soy sauce)
Fresh or dried oregano, to taste
Ground black pepper

**1.** Mix the salad ingredients together, reserving a few pumpkin seeds and spring onions for garnishing.

**2.** Shake the dressing ingredients together in a screw-topped jar.

**3.** Pour over the salad and mix gently.

TIME: Preparation takes 20 minutes.

SERVING IDEA: Serve with a lettuce salad.
Wheatberries also mix well with grated carrot and an orange dressing.

COOK'S TIP: This salad keeps well so it can be made in advance and kept in the refrigerator until required.

# Spinach Salad

*Serve with a simple main course.*

*SERVES 4-6*

450g/1lb spinach
1 medium red cabbage
1 medium onion
100g/4oz apricots
6 tbsps French dressing
50g/2oz toasted sunflower seeds

**1.** Wash the spinach and drain well.

**2.** First remove the outer leaves and core, then slice the cabbage finely.

**3.** Slice the onion finely and cut the apricots into slivers.

**4.** Tear the spinach leaves with the fingers into bite-sized pieces and put into a serving dish.

**5.** Add the sliced cabbage, onion and apricots.

**6.** Pour over the dressing and mix together thoroughly.

**7.** Sprinkle with sunflower seeds and serve.

TIME: Preparation takes 15 minutes.

WATCHPOINT: Spinach leaves bruise easily so take care when washing and tearing the leaves.

COOK'S TIP: If using dried apricots, soak beforehand in a little fruit juice.

# SMOKED TOFU SALAD

*A tasty main course salad. Serve with granary bread.*

*SERVES 4-6*

225g/8oz broccoli florets
100g/4oz mushrooms
100g/4oz pineapple
4 tbsps sweetcorn
4-6 tbsps French dressing
1 packet smoked tofu, cut into cubes

**1.** Cover the broccoli florets with boiling water and leave to stand for 5 minutes. Drain and allow to cool.

**2.** Wipe the mushrooms with a clean cloth and slice thinly.

**3.** Cut the pineapple into small pieces.

**4.** Put the broccoli, mushrooms, pineapple and sweetcorn into a large bowl together with the French dressing.

**5.** Mix carefully.

**6.** Divide the salad between 4 individual dishes and place the smoked tofu on top.

**7.** Serve at once.

TIME: Preparation takes 15 minutes.

VARIATION: Omit the tofu and serve as a side salad with savoury flans.

COOK'S TIP: If using plain tofu, marinate for a few hours in equal parts of shoyu sauce and olive oil, together with 1 crushed clove of garlic and 1 tsp of fresh grated ginger.

# SEELI SALAD

*Serve this very attractive salad for a party or as part of a buffet.*

*SERVES 4-6*

1 large red cabbage
1 green pepper, de-seeded and chopped
½ small pineapple, peeled and finely
    chopped
Segments from 2 medium oranges
6 spring onions, finely chopped
3 sticks celery, chopped
75g/3oz hazelnuts, roughly chopped
75g/3oz sprouted aduki beans

*Dressing*
100ml/4fl.oz mayonnaise
50ml/2fl.oz Greek yogurt
Seasoning

**1.** Remove any tough or discoloured outer leaves from the cabbage.

**2.** Remove the base so that the cabbage will stand upright, and cut about a quarter off the top.

**3.** Using a sharp knife, scoop out the inside of the cabbage leaving 0.6cm/¼" for the shell. Set the shell aside.

**4.** Discard any tough pieces and shred the remaining cabbage very finely.

**5.** Put the shredded cabbage into a large bowl together with the pepper, pineapple, orange segments, spring onions, celery, hazelnuts and beans.

**6.** Mix the mayonnaise, yogurt and seasoning together and carefully fold into the vegetables and fruit.

**7.** Put the mixture into the cabbage shell and place on a serving dish garnished with parsley.

TIME: Preparation takes 20 minutes.

WATCHPOINT: If preparing in advance, refrigerate the salad and dressing separately and mix them together just before serving.

VARIATION: Walnuts may be used in place of hazelnuts but add them when mixing the salad and dressing together.

# Sprouted Lentil Salad

*A quick and easy salad.*

*SERVES 4-6*

225g/8oz broccoli florets
1 red pepper
225g/8oz sprouted lentils
50g/2oz sultanas
4-6 tbsps French dressing
1 tsp freshly grated ginger

**1.** Cover the broccoli florets with boiling water and leave to stand for 5 minutes. Drain and cool.

**2.** Core and de-seed the pepper and dice roughly.

**3.** Arrange the sprouted lentils on a serving dish.

**4.** Mix together the broccoli florets, pepper and sultanas and pile in the centre.

**5.** Mix the grated ginger with the French dressing and pour over the salad.

**6.** Serve at once.

TIME: Preparation takes 15 minutes.

SERVING IDEA: Serve with pastry based dishes.

VARIATION: Cauliflower florets may be used in place of broccoli.

# MOUNT CARMEL SALAD

*Serve as an accompaniment to a hot main dish.*

*SERVES 4-6*

100g/4oz carrots, peeled
1 green pepper
50g/2oz apricots
1 tbsp sesame seeds
225g/8oz beansprouts
4 tbsps French dressing
2 tbsps pineapple juice

**1.** Cut the carrots into matchsticks.

**2.** De-seed and slice the pepper thinly.

**3.** Cut the apricots into slivers.

**4.** Toast the sesame seeds in a dry pan over a low heat until they are golden brown and give off a delicious aroma.

**5.** Place the carrots, pepper, apricots and beansprouts in a serving dish.

**6.** Mix the French dressing with the pinapple juice and fold into the salad.

**7.** Sprinkle the sesame seeds over the top.

**8.** Serve at once.

TIME: Preparation takes 10 minutes.

COOK'S TIP: Use beansprouts which are at least 2.5cm/1–inch long for this recipe.

# INDIAN VEGETABLE CURRY

*A wonderfully tasty curry which has the added
advantage of freezing well.*

*SERVES 4*

*Spices*
2 tsps turmeric
1 tsp cummin
1 tsp mustard seed
1 tsp fenugreek
4 tsps coriander
½ tsp chilli powder
1 tsp ginger
1 tsp black peppercorns

1lb onions, finely chopped
Ghee or vegetable oil (vary amount to suit
  – about 4 tbsps)
½ pint sterilised milk
2 tbsps white wine vinegar
400g/14oz tin tomatoes, liquidised with
  their juice
1 tbsp tomato purée
2 tsps brown sugar
1 tsp vegetable bouillon powder or 1
  stock cube dissolved in little boiling
  water
900g/2lbs chopped mushrooms or mixed
vegetables (e.g. mushrooms, cauliflower,
carrots, potatoes, okra)

**1.** Grind all the spices together, this amount will make 3 tbsps of curry powder.

**2.** Fry the onions in the ghee or vegetable oil until golden.

**3.** Add the ground spices, lower the heat and cook for 3 minutes, stirring all the time.

**4.** Add the milk and vinegar and stir well.

**5.** Add the liquidised tomatoes, tomato purée, sugar and stock.

**6.** Bring to the boil, cover and simmer very gently for 1 hour.

**7.** Add the vegetables and cook until tender – about 30 minutes.

TIME: Preparation takes 30 minutes, cooking takes 1 hour 30 minutes.

SERVING IDEA: Serve with boiled brown rice, chapattis and Cucumber Raita. Cucumber Raita – combine diced cucumber with yogurt, a little chopped mint, a pinch of chilli powder, cumin and seasoning to taste.

FREEZING: The curry sauce will freeze well for up to 3 months so it is well worth while making double the quantity.

# SWEETCORN AND PARSNIP FLAN

*Serve this unusual flan with jacket potatoes
filled with cottage cheese and chives.*

*SERVES 6*

*Base*
75g/3oz soft margarine
175g/6oz wholemeal flour
1 tsp baking powder
Pinch of salt
4-6 tbsps ice-cold water
1 tbsp oil

*Filling*
1 large onion, peeled and finely chopped
1 clove garlic, crushed
25g/1oz butter or margarine
2 large parsnips, steamed and roughly
   mashed
175g/6oz sweetcorn, frozen or tinned
1 tsp dried basil
Salt and pepper
3 eggs
140ml/¼ pint milk
75g/3oz grated Cheddar cheese
1 medium tomato, sliced ·

**1.** Rub the margarine into the flour, baking powder and salt until the mixture resembles fine breadcrumbs.

**2.** Add the water and oil and work together lightly. The mixture should be fairly moist.

**3.** Leave aside for half an hour.

**4.** Roll out and line a 25.4cm/10 inch flan dish.

**5.** Prick the bottom and bake blind at 210°C/425°F/Gas Mark 7 for about 8 minutes.

**6.** Meanwhile, sauté the onion and garlic in the butter or margarine until soft and golden.

**7.** Add the parsnips, sweetcorn and basil and season to taste.

**8.** Beat the eggs and add the milk.

**9.** Add to the vegetable mixture and stir over a low heat until the mixture just begins to set.

**10.** Pour into the flan base and top with the grated cheese and sliced tomato.

**11.** Bake 190°C/375°F/Gas Mark 5 for 20 minutes, until the cheese is golden brown.

TIME: Preparation takes about 40 minutes, cooking takes 30 minutes.

COOK'S TIP: The partial cooking of the whole mixture before placing in the flan base helps to keep the base from becoming soggy and considerably reduces the cooking time.

# SWEET POTATO AND FRENCH BEAN PASTIES

*These pasties are a tasty addition to any lunch box or picnic basket.*

*SERVES 4*

225g/8oz wholemeal shortcrust pastry
½ medium onion, finely chopped
1 clove garlic, crushed
1 tbsp oil
½ tsp freshly grated ginger
¼ – ½ tsp chilli powder
¼ tsp turmeric
½ tsp ground cumin
1 tsp ground coriander
¼ tsp mustard powder
1 medium-sized sweet potato, cooked and
   finely diced
100g/4oz French beans, chopped into
   1.2cm/½ -inch lengths
2 tbsps water or stock
Salt and pepper

**1.** Fry the onion and garlic in the oil until soft.

**2.** Add the ginger and all the spices and stir.

**3.** Add the diced potato, beans and water or stock, and cook gently for 4-5 minutes, or until the beans begin to cook.

**4.** Allow the mixture to cool and season well.

**5.** Roll out the pastry into 4 circles.

**6.** Place a quarter of the filling in the centre of each circle and dampen the edges of the pastry with a little water.

**7.** Join the pastry together over the filling.

**8.** Make a small hole in each pasty and glaze with milk or egg.

**9.** Bake for 15-20 minutes at 200°C/400°F/ Gas Mark 6.

TIME: Preparation, including making the pastry, takes 25 minutes.
Cooking takes 15-20 minutes.

FREEZING: The pasties will freeze well for up to 2 months. Thaw at room temperature.

# CARROT AND CASHEW NUT ROAST

*A delicious roast to serve hot, but the full flavour of*
*the caraway seeds and lemon are more prominent*
*when the roast is served cold.*

*SERVES 6*

1 medium-sized onion, chopped
1-2 cloves garlic, crushed
1 tbsp olive or sunflower oil
450g/1lb carrots, cooked and mashed
225g/8oz cashew nuts, ground
100g/4oz wholewheat breadcrumbs
1 tbsp light tahini
1½ tsps caraway seeds
1 tsp yeast extract
Juice of ½ a lemon
2½ fl.oz/65ml stock from the carrots or
   water
Salt and pepper

**1.** Fry the onion and garlic in the oil until soft.

**2.** Mix together with all the other ingredients and season to taste.

**3.** Place the mixture in a greased 900g/2lb loaf tin.

**4.** Cover with foil and bake at 180°C/350°F/Gas Mark 4 for 1 hour.

**5.** Remove the foil and bake for a further 10 minutes.

**6.** Leave to stand in the baking tin for at least 10 minutes before turning out.

TIME: Preparation takes 20 minutes, cooking takes 1 hour 10 minutes.

FREEZING: This loaf can be frozen at the end of Step 3. When required, remove from the freezer and thaw overnight in the refrigerator then continue from Step 4 or freeze at the end of Step 6.

SERVING IDEA: Serve hot with roast potatoes and a green vegetable, or cold with a mixed green salad.

# PERFECT POTATOES

*Potatoes become extra special when teamed
up with the flavour of onion.*

*SERVES 5*

900g/2lbs potatoes
1 large onion
Salt and pepper
280ml/½ pint milk
40g/1½ oz butter or margarine

**1.** Peel and finely slice the potatoes and onion.

**2.** Layer the potato slices and onion in a shallow ovenproof dish, sprinkling each layer with some salt and pepper.

**3.** Pour over the milk and dot with the butter or margarine.

**4.** Bake uncovered in a preheated oven, 180°C/350°F/Gas Mark 4 for 1-1½ hours or until the potatoes are soft, golden and brown on top.

TIME: Preparation takes 15 minutes, cooking takes 1-1½ hours.

SERVING IDEA: Serve with grilled mushrooms and tomatoes for a supper dish or serve with roasts, burgers or pies.

FREEZING: Cook quickly, cover with foil and place in a freezer bag. Thaw at room temperature for 4-6 hours and reheat at 190°C/375°F/Gas Mark 5 for about 30 minutes.

VARIATION: Place a layer of finely sliced cooking apples in the bottom of the dish.

# DEEP MUSHROOM PIE

*A delicious pie and so adaptable. Serve with*
*salad or potatoes and a green vegetable.*

*SERVES 4*

*Filling*
1 tbsp vegetable oil
2 medium onions, peeled and finely
  chopped
350g/¾ lb mushrooms, cleaned and
  chopped
225g/8oz mixed nuts, finely milled
100g/4oz wholewheat breadcrumbs
2 eggs, beaten
1 tsp dried thyme or 2 tsps fresh
1 tsp dried marjoram or 2 tsps fresh
1 tbsps shoyu (Japanese soy sauce)
Salt and pepper to taste
Small quantity of stock or water if
  necessary

*Pastry*
350g/12oz wholewheat flour
Pinch of salt
1 tsp baking powder (optional)
100g/4oz solid vegetable fat
100ml/4fl.oz water plus extra boiling
  water as necessary
Beaten egg to glaze

**1.** Heat the oil in a large saucepan and gently fry the onion until soft.

**2.** Add the finely chopped mushrooms and cook until the juices begin to run.

**3.** Remove from the heat and add all the other filling ingredients to form a thick, but not dry, consistency, adding a little stock or water if necessary. Allow to cool.

**4.** To prepare the pastry, first sift the flour, salt and baking powder into a large mixing bowl.

**5.** Cut the fat into small pieces and melt in a saucepan. Add the cold water and bring to a fierce, bubbling boil.

**6.** Immediately pour into the centre of the flour and mix vigorously with a wooden spoon until glossy.

**7.** When the mixture is cool enough to handle, knead it into a ball.

**8.** Divide the mixture into two-thirds and one-third, placing the one-thirds portion in an oiled plastic bag to prevent drying out.

**9.** Use the two-thirds portion to line the base and sides of a 19cm/7–inch spring mould, pressing it down and moulding it into position.

**10.** Spoon in the mushroom filling, press down firmly making a 'dome' shape.

**11.** Roll out the remaining pastry to just larger than the tin and place on top of the pie, pinching the edges together to seal.

**12.** Trim off excess pastry and glaze generously with beaten egg.

**13.** Cut or prick vents in the lid to allow the steam to escape.

**14.** Bake at 220°C/425°F/Gas Mark 7 for 20 minutes. Reduce to 190°C/375°F/Gas Mark 5 and bake for a further hour.

**15.** Unmould and serve on an attractive platter surrounded by watercress and twists of lemon and cucumber.

TIME: Preparation takes about 35 minutes, cooking takes 1 hour 20 minutes.

# NUTTY SPAGHETTI

*Serve this easy-to-make dish with French bread for a tasty mid-week meal.*

*SERVES 4*

225g/8oz spaghetti
710ml/1¼ pints boiling, salted water
1 onion, finely chopped
2 tbsps sunflower oil
2½ tsps curry powder
175ml/6fl.oz tomato juice
3 tbsps crunchy peanut butter
1 tbsp lemon juice
Lemon twists and peanuts for garnish

**1.** Boil the spaghetti in the salted water until just tender, and drain well.

**2.** Fry the onion in the oil until golden brown.

**3.** Stir in the curry powder, tomato juice, peanut butter and lemon juice.

**4.** Simmer for 5 minutes and then stir into the spaghetti.

TIME: Preparation takes about 10 minutes, cooking takes 25 minutes.

SERVING IDEA: Serve garnished with lemon twists and peanuts.

VARIATION: Almond butter and blanched almonds can be used in place of the peanut butter and peanuts.

# RATATOUILLE LASAGNE

*Serve with crusty rolls and a green salad – perfect for
informal entertaining.*

*SERVES 4-6*

6 strips lasagne verdi or wholemeal
   lasagne
2-3 tbsps olive oil
2 onions, finely chopped
2 cloves garlic, crushed
1 large aubergine, chopped
1 courgette, sliced thinly
1 green pepper, chopped
1 red pepper, chopped
400g/14oz tin tomatoes, chopped
2-3 tbsps tomato purée
A little vegetable stock
Salt and freshly ground black pepper

*White sauce*
25g/1oz butter or margarine
25g/1oz wholemeal flour
280ml/½ pint milk

40g/1½ oz Parmesan cheese, grated
Parsley, to garnish

**1.** Preheat the oven to 180°C/350°F/Gas
Mark 4.

**2.** Cook the lasagne in boiling, salted
water for 12-15 minutes.

**3.** Plunge into a bowl of cold water to
prevent overcooking or sticking.

**4.** Heat the oil and fry the onion and
garlic until soft.

**5.** Add the aubergine, courgette and
peppers and sauté until soft.

**6.** Add the tomatoes with their juice and
the tomato purée, and simmer until
tender. It may be necessary to add a little
stock at this stage.

**7.** Season well and set aside.

**8.** Make the white sauce by melting the
butter in a small saucepan.

**9.** Add the flour and cook to a roux.

**10.** Add the milk slowly, stirring
constantly. Bring to the boil and simmer
for about 5 minutes. Remove from the
heat.

**11.** Grease a deep ovenproof dish.

**12.** Layer the ratatouille and lasagne strips,
starting with the ratatouille and finishing
with a layer of lasagne.

**13.** Pour over the white sauce and
sprinkle the Parmesan cheese over the
top.

**14.** Bake in the oven for 35 minutes until
golden. Garnish with parsley before
serving.

TIME: Preparation takes about 20 minutes, cooking takes 1 hour.

VARIATION: If aubergine is not available, 225g/8oz sliced mushrooms may be used instead.

# COURGETTE AND CARROT LAYER

*Serve with a sprouted salad and new potatoes, or glaze
with agar and fresh herbs for a special occasion.*

*SERVES 4*

450g/1lb carrots, cooked, mashed and
    seasoned
1 medium onion
450g/1lb courgettes, finely chopped
1 tbsp oil
100g/4oz almonds, finely chopped or
    ground
75g/3oz wholemeal breadcrumbs
1 tsp Vecon (vegetable stock) dissolved in
    a little boiling water
1 egg, beaten
1 level tsp mixed herbs
1 tbsp tomato purée
1 tbsp shoyu sauce (Japanese soy sauce)
Ground black pepper

**1.** Grease and line a 450g/1lb loaf tin.

**2.** Fry the onion and courgettes in the oil, add all the remaining ingredients except the carrot, and mix together well.

**3.** Place half of the courgette mixture into the loaf tin and press down well.

**4.** Arrange the carrots on top of this followed by the remaining courgette mixture.

**5.** Cover with foil and cook for 1 hour at 175°C/350°F/Gas Mark 4

**6.** Allow to cool for 10 minutes before removing from tin.

TIME: Preparation, including cooking the carrots, takes 25 minutes.

COOK'S TIP: This mixture makes a delicious filling for a raised pie.

# WINTER CRUMBLE

*A variety of hearty vegetables topped with oats and
cheese makes the perfect winter meal.*

*SERVES 4-6*

*Topping*
75g/3oz butter or margarine
100g/4oz wholewheat flour
50g/2oz rolled oats
100g/4oz Cheddar cheese, grated
¼ tsp salt

175ml/6fl.oz stock or water
280ml/½ pint sweet cider
1 tsp brown sugar
2 carrots, chopped
2 large parsnips, cut into rings
2 sticks celery, chopped
2 heads broccoli, cut into florets
¼ cauliflower, cut into florets
1 dstsp wholewheat flour
2 tbsps chopped parsley
1 medium onion, chopped and fried until
   golden
4 large tomatoes, peeled and sliced
225g/8oz cooked black-eyed beans
Salt and pepper

**1.** Make the topping by rubbing the butter into the flour and oats until the mixture resembles fine breadcrumbs.

**2.** Stir in the cheese and salt.

**3.** Mix the stock with the cider and sugar and put into a large pan with the carrots and parsnips.

**4.** Cook until just tender, remove the vegetables and put aside.

**5.** Add the celery, broccoli and cauliflower to the pan, cook until tender, remove and reserve with other vegetables.

**6.** Mix the flour with a little water, add to the cider and cook until thickened, stirring all the time.

**7.** Cook for 2-3 minutes, remove from the heat and add the parsley.

**8.** Place the onions, vegetables, tomatoes and beans in a greased casserole and season well. Pour the sauce over the mixture.

**9.** Sprinkle the topping over the top and press down a little.

**10.** Cook at 200°C/400°F/Gas mark 6 for 30-35 minutes or until the topping is golden brown.

TIME: Preparation takes 20 minutes, cooking takes 1 hour 5 minutes.

SERVING IDEA: Serve with roast potatoes.

COOK'S TIP: The casserole can be prepared in advance to the end of Step 9. Refrigerate until ready to cook.

# SAVOURY BEAN POT

*Serve this exciting mixture with rice or jacket potatoes and a salad.*

*SERVES 4*

2 tbsps vegetable oil
2 vegetable stock cubes, crumbled
2 medium onions, chopped
2 eating apples, peeled and grated
2 medium carrots, grated
3 tbsps tomato purée
280ml/½ pint water
2 tbsps white wine vinegar
1 tbsp dried mustard
1 level tsp oregano
1 level tsp cumin
1 dstsp brown sugar
Salt and pepper
450g/1lb cooked red kidney beans
A little soured cream

**1.** Heat the oil in a non-stick pan.

**2.** Add the crumbled stock cubes, onions, apples and carrots.

**3.** Sauté for 5 minutes, stirring continuously.

**4.** Mix the tomato purée with the water and add together with all the other ingredients apart from the beans and cream.

**5.** Stir well, cover and simmer for 2 minutes.

**6.** Add the beans and tip the mixture into an ovenproof casserole.

**7.** Cover and cook at 180°C/350°F/Gas Mark 4 for 35-40 minutes.

**8.** Add a little more water after 20 minutes if necessary.

**9.** Top with swirls of soured cream and serve.

TIME: Preparation takes 20 minutes, cooking takes 45 minutes.

VARIATION: Use cider vinegar in place of the white wine vinegar.

# TOMATO AND PEPPER QUICHE

*Quiche is tastiest served with jacket potatoes and a crisp salad.*

*SERVES 4*

*Pastry case*
100g/4oz wholewheat flour
Pinch of salt
50g/2oz vegetable fat
A little cold water to mix

*Filling*
25g/1oz butter or margarine
1 onion, finely chopped
½ green pepper, finely sliced
½ red pepper, finely sliced
2 tomatoes, finely sliced
3 eggs
280ml/½ pint single cream
Seasoning
2 tbsps Parmesan cheese

**1.** Mix the flour and salt together.

**2.** Cut the fat into small pieces and rub into the flour until the mixture resembles fine breadcrumbs.

**3.** Add the water and mix until a ball of dough is formed.

**4.** Roll out to line a 20cm/8 inch flan tin or quiche dish.

**5.** Prick the bottom lightly with a fork and cook at 180°C/350°F/Gas Mark 4 for 15 minutes.

**6.** Remove from the oven.

**7.** Meanwhile, melt the butter or margarine in a frying pan and sauté the onion and peppers until just softened.

**8.** Arrange the onion and peppers on the bottom of the pastry case followed by the sliced tomatoes.

**9.** Beat the eggs, and add the cream and seasoning.

**10.** Pour over the vegetables and sprinkle the cheese on top.

**11.** Return to the oven for 35-40 minutes until risen and golden brown on top.

TIME: Preparation takes 25 minutes, cooking takes 55 minutes.

VARIATION: For an everyday quiche, replace the cream with milk.

# VEGETABLE STEW WITH HERB DUMPLINGS

*The ideal meal to warm up a cold winter's night.*

*SERVES 4-6*

1 large onion
900g/2lbs mixed vegetables (carrot,
    swede, parsnips, turnips,
    cauliflower etc.)
570ml/1 pint vegetable stock
Salt and pepper
Flour or proprietory gravy powder to
    thicken

*Dumplings*
100g/4oz wholewheat self-raising flour
50g/2oz vegetarian suet
1 tsp mixed herbs
¼ tsp salt

**1.** Chop the onion into large pieces.

**2.** Peel and prepare the vegetables and chop into bite-sized pieces.

**3.** Put the onion and vegetables into a pan and cover with the stock.

**4.** Bring to the boil and simmer for 20 minutes.

**5.** Season to taste.

**6.** Mix a little flour or gravy powder with a little water and stir into the stew to thicken.

**7.** Place the ingredients for the dumplings into a bowl and add just enough water to bind.

**8.** Shape the mixture into 8 small dumplings.

**9.** Bring the stew to the boil and drop in the dumplings.

**10.** Cover and allow to simmer for 10 minutes.

**11.** Serve at once.

TIME: Preparation takes 10 minutes, cooking takes 30 minutes.

SERVING IDEA: Serve with boiled potatoes.

VARIATION: The mixed herbs may be omitted when making the dumplings or chopped fresh parsley and a squeeze of lemon juice may be used instead.

# SAVOURY RICE CAKE

*An excellent way to use up left-over rice.*

*SERVES 2-4*

1 medium onion, finely chopped
1 clove garlic, crushed
2 tbsps olive oil
1 tbsp fresh thyme, chopped
1 red pepper, thinly sliced
1 green pepper, thinly sliced
4 eggs, beaten
Salt and pepper
6 tbsps cooked brown rice
3 tbsps natural yogurt
75g/3oz Cheddar cheese, grated

**1.** Fry the onion and garlic in the olive oil until soft.

**2.** Add the thyme and peppers and fry gently for 4-5 minutes.

**3.** Beat the eggs with the salt and pepper.

**4.** Add the cooked rice to the thyme and peppers followed by the eggs.

**5.** Cook over a moderate heat, stirring from time to time until the eggs are cooked underneath.

**6.** Spoon the yogurt on top of the part-set egg and sprinkle the cheese over the top.

**7.** Put under a moderate grill and cook until puffed and golden.

**8.** Serve immediately.

TIME: Preparation takes about 15 minutes, cooking takes 15 minutes.

SERVING IDEA: Garnish with fresh thyme and serve with a green salad.

# COURGETTES MEDITERRANEAN STYLE

*Any other type of cooked bean may be used for this dish.*

*SERVES 4*

3 tbsps olive oil
1 large onion, finely chopped
3 cloves garlic, crushed
1 red pepper, chopped
225g/8oz cooked haricot beans
400g/14oz tin tomatoes
450g/1lb courgettes, finely sliced
1 level tsp oregano
Seasoning

**1.** Heat the oil in a pan.

**2.** Add the onion, garlic and pepper and cook for 4-5 minutes.

**3.** Add the cooked beans, tinned tomatoes and courgettes. Stir well.

**4.** Add the oregano and seasoning, and stir again.

**5.** Cover and cook slowly for 30 minutes.

TIME: Preparation takes 10-15 minutes, cooking takes 40 minutes.

SERVING IDEA: Serve on a bed of white rice.

COOK'S TIP: This dish will reheat well.

# LENTIL MOUSSAKA

*Try a taste of the Greek Islands with this classic dish.*

*SERVES 4-6*

150g/5oz green lentils
1 large aubergine, sliced
4-5 tbsps oil
1 large onion, chopped
1 clove garlic, crushed
1 large carrot, diced
4 sticks celery, finely chopped
1-2 tsps mixed herbs
400g/14oz tin tomatoes
1 dstsp shoyu sauce (Japanese soy sauce)
Black pepper
2 medium potatoes, cooked and sliced
2 large tomatoes, sliced

*Sauce*
50g/2oz margarine
50g/2oz brown rice flour
425ml/¾ pint milk
1 large egg, separated
50g/2oz grated Cheddar cheese
1 tsp nutmeg

**1.** Cook the lentils in plenty of water until soft. Drain and reserve the liquid.

**2.** Fry the aubergine in the oil, drain well and set aside.

**3.** Sauté the onion, garlic, carrot, celery and add a little of the lentil stock.

**4.** Simmer with the lid on until just tender.

**5.** Add the lentils, mixed herbs and tinned tomatoes. Simmer gently for 3-4 minutes.

**6.** Season with the shoyu and pepper.

**7.** Place a layer of the lentil mixture in a large casserole dish and cover with half of the aubergine slices.

**8.** Cover the aubergine slices with half of the potato slices and all the tomatoes.

**9.** Repeat with the remaining lentils, aubergines and potatoes.

**10.** To make the sauce, melt the margarine in a saucepan, remove from the heat and stir in the flour to make a roux. Return to a gentle heat for 1-2 minutes.

**11.** Add the milk gradually, blending well, so that the sauce is smooth and lump free. Stir continually until the sauce thickens.

**12.** Remove the pan from the heat and cool slightly. Add the egg yolk, stir in the cheese and add the nutmeg.

**13.** Beat the egg white until it is stiff, then carefully fold into the sauce.

**14.** Pour the sauce over the moussaka, covering the dish completely.

**15.** Bake at 180°C/350°F/Gas Mark 4 for about 40 minutes until the top is golden brown and puffy.

TIME: Preparation takes 45 minutes, cooking takes 1 hour 10 minutes

SERVING IDEA: Serve with a crunchy green salad or battered mushrooms.

# VEGETARIAN PAELLA

*Perfect served with crusty bread and a green salad.*

*SERVES 4-6*

60ml/4 tbsps olive oil
1 large onion, chopped
2 cloves garlic, crushed
½ tsp paprika
350g/12oz long grain brown rice
850ml/1½ pints stock
175ml/6fl.oz dry white wine
400g/14oz tin tomatoes, plus juice,
   chopped
1 tbsp tomato purée
½ tsp tarragon
1 tsp basil
1 tsp oregano
1 red pepper, roughly chopped
1 green pepper, roughly chopped
3 sticks celery, finely chopped
225g/8oz mushrooms, washed and sliced
50g/2oz mange tout, topped and tailed
  and cut into halves
100g/4oz frozen peas
50g/2oz cashew nut pieces
Salt and pepper
Parsley, lemon wedges and olives to garnish

**1.** Heat the oil and fry the onion and garlic until soft.

**2.** Add the paprika and rice and continue to cook for 4-5 minutes until the rice is transparent. Stir occasionally.

**3.** Add the stock, wine, tomatoes, tomato purée and herbs and simmer for 10-15 minutes.

**4.** Add the peppers, celery, mushrooms and mange tout and continue to cook for another 30 minutes until the rice is cooked.

**5.** Add the peas, cashew nuts and seasoning to taste.

**6.** Heat through and place on a large heated serving dish.

**7.** Sprinkle the parsley over the top and garnish with lemon wedges and olives.

TIME: Preparation takes 20 minutes, cooking takes 45 minutes.

COOK'S TIP: To prepare in advance, undercook slightly, add a little more stock or water and reheat. Do not add the peas until just before serving otherwise they will lose their colour.

# ASPARAGUS AND OLIVE QUICHE

*An interesting combination which gives
a new twist to a classic dish.*

*MAKES 2 x 10 INCH QUICHES*

2 x 25cm/10 inch part baked pastry shells
6 eggs
570ml/1 pint single cream
1 tsp salt
Pinch of nutmeg
Salt and pepper
2 tbsps flour
2 tins green asparagus tips
175g/6oz green olives
2 onions, finely chopped and sautéed in a
   little butter until soft
75g/3oz Cheddar cheese, grated
2 tbsps Parmesan cheese
50g/2oz butter

**1.** Whisk the eggs with the cream.

**2.** Add the salt, nutmeg and seasoning.

**3.** Mix a little of the mixture with the flour until smooth, then add to the cream mixture.

**4.** Arrange the asparagus tips, olives and onion in the pastry shells and pour the cream mixture over the top.

**5.** Sprinkle with the grated Cheddar and Parmesan.

**6.** Dot with the butter and bake at 190°C/375°F/Gas Mark 5 for 25 minutes.

**7.** Turn down the oven to 180°C/350°F/Gas Mark 4 for a further 15 minutes until the quiches are golden.

TIME: Preparation takes 20 minutes, cooking takes 40 minutes.

FREEZING: The quiches may be frozen but a slightly better result is obtained if you freeze the pastry shells and add the filling just before baking.

# SAVOURY GRAIN CASSEROLE

*Serve as a complete meal for two people or serve*
*accompanied with lightly steamed vegetables for four people.*

*SERVES 2-4*

75g/3oz brown rice
75g/3oz split peas
2 sticks celery, very finely chopped
1 medium onion, very finely chopped
100g/4oz mushrooms, chopped
400g/14oz tin tomatoes, drained and
    chopped or 225g/8oz tomatoes, peeled
    and chopped
½ tsp dill seeds
½ tsp thyme
2 tbsps shoyu sauce (Japanese soy sauce)
1 egg, beaten
100g/4oz Cheddar cheese, grated

**1.** Cover the rice with water and cook for 10-15 minutes; drain.

**2.** Cover the split peas with water and cook for 20 minutes until just tender but not mushy; drain.

**3.** Meanwhile, combine the celery, onion, mushrooms, tomatoes, dill, thyme, shoyu and the egg in a large bowl.

**4.** Stir in the rice and peas.

**5.** Place the mixture in a greased ovenproof casserole dish and cook for 45 minutes at 180°C/350°F/Gas Mark 4.

**6.** Remove from the oven and sprinkle with the grated cheese.

**7.** Return to the oven for 10 minutes until the cheese has melted.

**8.** Serve at once.

TIME: Preparation takes 10 minutes, cooking takes 1 hour 45 minutes.

SERVING IDEA: Garnish with a few whole cooked button mushrooms or grilled tomatoes.

# VEGETARIAN SHEPHERD'S PIE

*This pie will serve two people without
any accompaniments and four people if served with vegetables.*

*SERVES 2-4*

100g/4oz brown lentils
50g/2oz pot barley
425ml/¾ pint stock or water
1 tsp yeast extract
1 large carrot, diced
½ onion, chopped finely
1 clove garlic, crushed
50g/2oz walnuts, roughly chopped
1 tsp vegetarian gravy powder or
   thickener
Salt and pepper
450g/1lb potatoes, cooked and mashed

**1.** Simmer the lentils and barley in 280ml/
½ pint of the stock and the yeast extract
for 30 minutes.

**2.** Meanwhile, cook the carrot, onion,
garlic and walnuts in the remaining stock
for 15 minutes or until tender.

**3.** Mix the gravy powder or thickener with
a little water and add to the carrot
mixture, stirring over a low heat until
thickened.

**4.** Combine the lentils and barley with the
carrot mixture, season and place in an
ovenproof dish.

**5.** Cover with the mashed potato and cook
at 180°C/350°F/Gas Mark 4 for about 30
minutes until browned on top.

TIME: Preparation takes 15 minutes, cooking takes 1 hour.

SERVING IDEA: Garnish with grilled tomatoes and serve with vegetables in season, such as
broccoli, sprouts, spring cabbage etc.

# BUTTER BEAN ONE-POT

*This is a quick to make, all-in-one dish.*

*SERVES 4*

2 tbsps vegetable oil
1 green pepper, finely chopped
1 large onion, finely chopped
2 sticks celery, diced
400g/14oz tin tomatoes
2 large potatoes, peeled and diced
280ml/½ pint vegetable stock or water
2 tbsps finely chopped parsley
Salt and pepper
450g/1lb cooked butter beans

**1.** Put the oil, pepper, onion and celery into a pan and cook gently until the onion begins to brown.

**2.** Add the tomatoes and their juice, plus the potatoes, stock, parsley, salt and pepper.

**3.** Simmer for about 30 minutes or until the liquid is reduced by half.

**4.** Add the beans and heat through gently for 5-10 minutes.

TIME: Preparation takes about 15 minutes, cooking takes 50 minutes.

SERVING IDEA: Serve with lots of crusty bread. Garlic bread also goes well with this dish.

VARIATION: To make a more substantial main course dish, follow the recipe to the end of instruction 3. Add the beans and stir well. Place in a casserole dish, top with a crumble mixture and bake in a hot oven for 25 minutes.

# TOFU BURGERS

*Serve these delicious burgers with mustard and
pickles and accompany with a salad.*

*MAKES 8*

50g/2oz bulgar wheat
100ml/4fl.oz boiling water
1 small onion, very finely chopped
50g/2oz carrot, grated
50g/2oz mushrooms, very finely chopped
250g/9oz packet tofu
½ tsp basil
½ tsp oregano
2 tbsps shoyu sauce (Japanese soy sauce)
1 tsp tomato purée
Black pepper
Wholewheat flour
Oil for deep frying

**1.** Put the bulgar wheat into a bowl and cover with boiling water. Leave to one side for 15 minutes until all the water has been absorbed.

**2.** Add the onion, carrot and mushrooms to the bulgar and mix well.

**3.** Drain the tofu and crumble into the bowl.

**4.** Add the basil, oregano, shoyu, tomato purée, a little black pepper and 1 tablespoon of wholewheat flour. Mix together well.

**5.** With wet hands, take heaped tablespoonful of the mixture, squeeze together well and shape into burgers.

**6.** Coat the burgers with wholewheat flour.

**7.** Heat the oil until very hot and fry the burgers 3 or 4 at a time until golden brown.

**8.** Remove and drain on absorbent kitchen paper.

TIME: Preparation takes 15 minutes, cooking takes 5 minutes per batch.

WATCHPOINT: The oil must be very hot otherwise the burgers will disintegrate.

FREEZING: It is well worth while doubling the quantity and freezing a batch of burgers. Freeze for up to 3 months. Reheat by grilling or warming in the oven.

# CAROB APPLE CAKE

*This cake is nicer if kept in an airtight tin for a day before serving.*

*MAKES 1 CAKE*

150g/5oz soft margarine
100g/4oz light muscovado sugar
1 large egg, beaten
175g/6oz fine wholemeal flour
60g/2½ oz light carob powder
1½ tsps baking powder
1 tbsp Amontillado sherry
400g/14oz Bramley cooking apples,
    peeled and sliced

*Topping*
75g/3oz carob chips
Knob of butter
A little water

**1.** Cream the margarine and sugar together
until fluffy.

**2.** Add half of the beaten egg and
continue creaming.

**3.** Add the rest of the egg together with
the sieved flour, carob and baking powder
and sherry.

**4.** Place half of the mixture into a round
17.8cm/8 inch cake tin and cover with the
sliced apples.

**5.** Add the other half of the mixture and
smooth the top.

**6.** Bake at 160°C/325°F/Gas Mark 3 for
1¼ hours or until firm to the touch.

**7.** Melt the carob chips with the butter and
water and drizzle over the top of the cake.

TIME: Preparation takes 25 minutes, cooking takes 1¼ hours.

SERVING IDEA: Serve hot with yogurt as a pudding or cold for afternoon tea.

# WINDWARD FRUIT BASKET

*An impressive dessert which is surprisingly easy to prepare.*

*SERVES 4-6*

1 large ripe melon
2 apples
Juice of 1 lime
2 mangoes
2 kiwi fruit
450g/1lb strawberries
225g/½ lb raspberries
3 tbsps honey
2 tbsps dark rum
50g/2oz butter

**1.** Cut the top off the melon and scoop out the seeds.

**2.** Using a melon baller, scoop out balls of melon and place in a large bowl.

**3.** Remove the core from the apples, dice and toss in the lime juice.

**4.** Peel and chop the mangoes.

**5.** Peel and slice the kiwi fruit.

**6.** Combine all the fruits.

**7.** Heat the honey, rum and butter gently until the butter has melted.

**8.** Cool, and pour over the fruits.

**9.** Toss gently and fill the melon shell with the fruit mixture.

**10.** Place on a serving dish and serve immediately.

TIME: Preparation takes 20 minutes, cooking takes 2 minutes.

SERVING IDEA: For a special occasion, make holes around the top of the melon with a skewer and decorated with fresh flowers.

VARIATION: Use any fresh fruits in season such pears, peaches etc.

# CRANBERRY AND APPLE CRUMBLE

*Serve hot with natural yogurt or serve cold with ice cream.*

*SERVES 4*

675g/1½ lbs Bramley or other cooking
    apples
50g/2oz raw cane sugar
175g/6oz fresh cranberries

*Crumble*
75g/3oz butter or margarine
50g/2oz sunflower seeds
75g/3oz raw cane or demerara sugar
150g/5oz wholewheat flour
50g/2oz Jumbo oats
50g/2oz porridge oats

**1.** Peel, core and dice the apples.

**2.** Place in a saucepan with the sugar and about 2 tbsps water.

**3.** Cook gently until just beginning to soften.

**4.** Add the cranberries and cook for a further minute. Remove from the heat.

**5.** Melt the butter or margarine in a small saucepan, add the sunflower seeds and fry very gently for a few minutes.

**6.** Meanwhile, mix together the other crumble ingredients in a bowl, rubbing in the sugar with the fingers if lumpy.

**7.** Pour the butter and sunflower seeds into this mixture and combine to form a loose crumble.

**8.** Place the fruit in a large, shallow oven-proof dish and sprinkle the crumble topping over.

**9.** Cook at 180°C/350°F/Gas Mark 4 for about 40 minutes or until the top is golden and crisp.

TIME: Preparation takes about 20 minutes, cooking takes 50 minutes.

# DE-LUXE BREAD AND BUTTER PUDDING

*Serve just as it is, hot from the oven.*

*SERVES 4*

4 thin slices wholemeal bread
A little butter
Raspberry jam
2 eggs, beaten
425ml/¾ pint milk, warmed
2 tbsps single cream
3 tbsps light muscovado sugar
1 tsp vanilla essence
2 tbsps sultanas, soaked for 1 hour
1 tbsp dates
Grated nutmeg

**1.** Remove the crusts from the bread.

**2.** Sandwich the bread with the butter and jam and cut into small triangles.

**3.** Beat the eggs until fluffy.

**4.** Add the warmed milk, cream, sugar and vanilla.

**5.** Stir together well, making sure that the sugar has dissolved.

**6.** Arrange the bread triangles in a lightly buttered ovenproof dish so that they overlap and stand up slightly.

**7.** Scatter the dried fruits over the top.

**8.** Pour the egg, cream and milk mixture into the dish, ensuring that the bread triangles are saturated.

**9.** Grate a little nutmeg over the pudding and bake at 200°C/400°F/Gas Mark 6 for about 30 minutes.

TIME: Preparation takes 10 minutes, cooking takes 30 minutes.

VARIATION: Other flavoured jams may be used instead of raspberry jam.

# Index

The publishers are indebted to The Vegetarian Society, Chris Hardisty, Freda Hooker, D.M. Arnot, Isabel A. Booth, Ian Jones, Marianne Vaney, Pam Knutson, Val Shaw, Susan Mills, Wendy Godden, Vivien Margison, Kate Allen and Sue Bliss.